Best Ever Knock Knock Jokes

FOR KIDS

Knock Knock
Who's there?
Luke.
Luke who?
Luke through the keyhole!

This edition published in 2023 by Arcturus Publishing Limited
26/27 Bickels Yard, 151–153 Bermondsey Street,
London SE1 3HA

Copyright © Arcturus Holdings Limited

All rights reserved. No part of this publication may be reproduced, stored in a retrieval system, or transmitted, in any form or by any means, electronic, mechanical, photocopying, recording, or otherwise, without prior written permission in accordance with the provisions of the Copyright Act 1956 (as amended). Any person or persons who do any unauthorized act in relation to this publication may be liable to criminal prosecution and civil claims for damages.

Illustrations: Luke Séguin-Magee
Editor: Donna Gregory
Designer: Marie Everitt

CH010507NT
Supplier 10, Date 0123, PI 00002700

Printed in the UK

Knock, knock...

Who's there?

Ben Hur.

Ben Hur who?

Ben Hur an hour—let me in!

Knock, knock...
Who's there?
Despair.
Despair who?
Despair room is full of junk!

Knock, knock...

Who's there?

Butternut.

Butternut who?

Butternut squash the eggs!

Knock, knock...

Who's there?

Chopin.

Chopin who?

Chopin in the supermarket.

Knock, knock...

Who's there?

Ivor.

Ivor who?

Ivor good mind not to tell you now!

Knock, knock...

Who's there?

Carmen.

Carmen who?

Carmen get it!

Knock, knock...

Who's there?

Isabelle.

Isabelle who?

Isabelle not a good idea?

Knock, knock...
Who's there?
Yul.
Yul who?
Yul soon see!

Knock, knock...
Who's there?
Max.
Max who?
Max no difference!

Knock, knock...
Who's there?
Army.
Army who?
Army aunts coming for dinner?

Knock, knock...
Who's there?
Fonda.
Fonda who?
Fonda you!

Knock, knock...

Who's there?

Alien.

Alien who?

Just how many aliens do you know?

Knock, knock...

Who's there?

Juno.

Juno who?

Juno the answer?

Knock, knock...

Who's there?

You are.

You are who?

I'm not Who, I'm me!

Knock, knock...

Who's there?

Buddha.

Buddha who?

Buddha this slice of bread for me!

Knock, knock...

Who's there?

Juicy.

Juicy who?

Juicy what I just saw?

Knock, knock...

Who's there?

Bach.

Bach who?

Bach to work, you slackers!

Knock, knock...

Who's there?

Honor Claire.

Honor Claire who?

Honor Claire day, you can see forever!

Knock, knock...

Who's there?

Ella Man.

Ella Man who?

Ella Man-tary, my dear Watson!

Knock, knock...

Who's there?

Dot.

Dot who?

Dots for me to know, and you to find out.

Knock, knock...

Who's there?

Ivor.

Ivor who?

Ivor sore hand from knocking!

Knock, knock...

Who's there?

Polly.

Polly who?

Polly door handle again, I think it's just stiff!

Knock, knock...

Who's there?

Arnie.

Arnie who?

Arnie ever going to let me in?

Knock, knock...

Who's there?

Phil.

Phil who?

Phil this bag with money, I'm a robber!

Knock, knock...

Who's there?

Sarah.

Sarah who?

Sarah phone I can use?

Knock, knock...

Who's there?

Elias.

Elias who?

Elias a terrible thing!

Knock, knock...

Who's there?

Arnold.

Arnold who?

Arnold friend you haven't seen for years!

Knock, knock...

Who's there?

Mabel.

Mabel who?

Mabel doesn't ring either!

Knock, knock...

Who's there?

Deanna.

Deanna who?

Deanna-mals are restless, don't go in the cages!

Knock, knock...

Who's there?

Freighter.

Freighter who?

I'm Freighter open the door!

Knock, knock...

Who's there?

Elsie.

Elsie who?

Elsie you around!

Knock, knock...

Who's there?

Lefty.

Lefty who?

Lefty home on your own again!

Knock, knock...

Who's there?

Spider.

Spider who?

Spider what everyone says, I like you!

Knock, knock...

Who's there?

Constance.

Constance who?

Constance snoring is keeping me awake!

Knock, knock...

Who's there?

Boliva.

Boliva who?

Boliva me, I know what I'm talking about!

Knock, knock...

Who's there?

Desi.

Desi who?

Designated hitter!

Knock, knock...

Who's there?

Vera.

Vera who?

Vera long way from home and need a map!

Knock, knock...

Who's there?

Igloo.

Igloo who?

Igloo knew Suzie like I know Suzie!

Knock, knock...

Who's there?

Willy.

Willy who?

Willy hurry up and let me in!

Knock, knock...

Who's there?

Major.

Major who?

Major mind up to open the door yet?

Knock, knock...

Who's there?

Hardy.

Hardy who?

Hardy har, fooled you!

Knock, knock...

Who's there?

Deena.

Deena who?

Deena hear me the first time?

Knock, knock...

Who's there?

Police.

Police who?

Police open the door and find out!

Knock, knock...

Who's there?

Aries.

Aries who?

Aries a reason I'm knocking at your door!

Knock, knock...

Who's there?

Reed.

Reed who?

Reed-turn to sender, address unknown!

Knock, knock...
Who's there?
Our Tell.
Our Tell who?
Our Tell you what I want, what I really really want!

Knock, knock...
Who's there?
Axl.
Axl who?
Axl me nicely and I might just tell you!

Knock, knock...
Who's there?
Veal chop.
Veal chop who?
Veal chop around and see vot bargains vee can pick up!

Knock, knock...
Who's there?
Esther.
Esther who?
Esther anything I can do for you?

Knock, knock...
Who's there?
Colin.
Colin who?
Colin the doctor, I feel ill!

Knock, knock...
Who's there?
Phil.
Phil who?
Phil this cup with sugar please. I've just run out!

Knock, knock...
Who's there?
Rosie.
Rosie who?
Rosie cheeks!

Knock, knock...
Who's there?
Butter.
Butter who?
Butter open quick, I have to go to the bathroom!

Knock, knock...

Who's there?

Mara.

Mara who?

Mara, Mara on the wall!

Knock, knock...
Who's there?
Cargo.
Cargo who?
Cargo beep! beep!

Knock, knock...

Who's there?

Superman.

Superman who?

You know I can't reveal my secret identity!

Knock, knock...

Who's there?

Ken.

Ken who?

Ken you come out to play?

Knock, knock...

Who's there?

Island.

Island who?

Island on your roof with my parachute!

Knock, knock...

Who's there?

Insurance salesman.

...

...hello...?
hello...?

Knock, knock...

Who's there?

Beethoven.

Beethoven who?

Beethoven is too hot!

Knock, knock...

Who's there?

Zombie.

Zombie who?

Zombies make honey, others are queens!

Knock, knock...

Who's there?

Eeyore.

Eeyore who?

Eeyore-ways keeps me waiting!

Knock, knock...

Who's there?

Nadia.

Nadia who?

Just Nadia head if you understand what I'm saying!

Knock, knock...
Who's there?
Hanover.
Hanover who?
Hanover your money!

Knock, knock...
Who's there?
Ammonia.
Ammonia who?
Ammonia little kid!

Knock, knock...
Who's there?
Theodore.
Theodore who?
Theodore wasn't open so I knocked!

Knock, knock...
Who's there?
Diesel.
Diesel who?
Diesel make you feel better!

Knock, knock...

Who's there?

Dan.

Dan who?

Dan just stand there—let me in!

Knock, knock...

Who's there?

Argo.

Argo who?

Argo to dance class after school!

Knock, knock...

Who's there?

Olive.

Olive who?

Olive you!

Knock, knock...
Who's there?
Gwen.
Gwen who?
Gwen are we going to get together?

Knock, knock...
Who's there?
Mae.
Mae who?
Mae be I'll tell you or maybe I won't!

Knock, knock
Who's there?
Cam.
Cam who?
Camelot is where King Arthur lived!

Knock, knock...
Who's there?
Arthur.
Arthur who?
Arthur any more cookies in the jar?

22

Knock, knock...

Who's there?

Who.

Who who?

Is there an owl in there?

Knock, knock...

Who's there?

Yah.

Yah who?

Yahoo! Ride 'em, cowboy!

Knock, knock...

Who's there?

Disk.

Disk who?

Disk is a recorded message, please leave your message after the beep!

Knock, knock...

Who's there?

Steve.

Steve who?

Steve upper lip!

Knock, knock...

Who's there?

Greta.

Greta who?

You Greta on my nerves!

Knock, knock...

Who's there?

Ina.

Ina who?

Ina minute I'm going to knock this door down!

Knock, knock...

Who's there?

Hammond.

Hammond who?

Hammond eggs for breakfast.

24

Knock, knock...

Who's there?

Queen.

Queen who?

Queen as a whistle!

Knock, knock...

Who's there?

Pizza.

Pizza who?

Pizza on Earth and goodwill to all men!

Knock, knock...

Who's there?

Congo.

Congo who?

Congo out, I'm grounded!

Knock, knock...

Who's there?

Alma.

Alma who?

Alma time seems to be spent on this doorstep!

Knock, knock...

Who's there?

Yootha.

Yootha who?

Yootha person with the bicycle for sale?

Knock, knock...

Who's there?

Willy.

Willy who?

Willy lend me a street map? I'm a stranger in town!

Knock, knock...

Who's there?

Hand.

Hand who?

Hand over your wallet, this is a raid!

Knock, knock...

Who's there?

Chile.

Chile who?

Chile out tonight, isn't it!

Knock, knock...

Who's there?

Violet.

Violet who?

Violet the cat out of the bag!

Knock, knock...

Who's there?

Ivan.

Ivan who?

Ivan idea you will know as soon as you open the door!

Knock, knock...

Who's there?

Ginger.

Ginger who?

Ginger hear the doorbell?

Knock, knock...

Who's there?

Cassie.

Cassie who?

Cassie the wood for the trees!

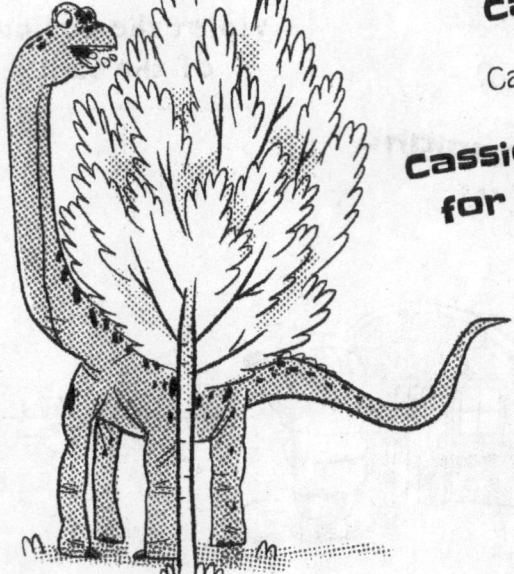

Knock, knock...

Who's there?

Cecile.

Cecile who?

Cecile th-the windows. Th-there's a m-monster out there.

Knock, knock...

Who's there?

Barry.

Barry who?

Barry the treasure then no one will find it!

Knock, knock...

Who's there?

Handel.

Handel who?

Handel with care!

Knock, knock...

Who's there?

Atilla.

Atilla who?

Atilla you open this door I'm a gonna stand here!

Knock, knock...

Who's there?

Banana.

Banana who?

Knock, knock...

Who's there?

Banana.

Banana who?

Knock, knock...

Who's there?

Orange.

Orange who?

Orange you glad I didn't say banana?

Knock, knock...

Who's there?

Joanna.

Joanna who?

Joanna have a guess?

Knock, knock...

Who's there?

Jaws.

Jaws who?

Jaws truly!

Knock, knock...

Who's there?

Albee.

Albee who?

Albee a monkey's uncle!

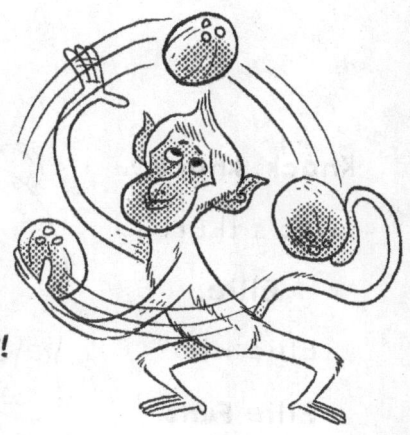

Knock, knock...

Who's there?

Jackson.

Jackson who?

Jackson the telephone, do you want to talk to him?

Knock, knock...

Who's there?

Tessa.

Tessa who?

Tessa long time for you to open the door!

Knock, knock...

Who's there?

Goat.

Goat who?

Goat to the door and find out!

Knock, knock...
Who's there?
Ellie.
Ellie who?
Ellie Funt.

Knock, knock...
Who's there?
Cliff.
Cliff who?
Cliff hanger!

Knock, knock...
Who's there?
Leaf.
Leaf who?
Leaf me alone!

Knock, knock...
Who's there?
Cow-go.
Cow-go who?
No, cow go MOO!!!

Knock, knock...

Who's there?

Soup.

Soup who?

Souperman!

Knock, knock...

Who's there?

Lettuce.

Lettuce who?

Lettuce in and you will find out!

Knock, knock...

Who's there?

Howl.

Howl who?

Howl you know unless you open the door?

33

Knock, knock...

Who's there?

Avon.

Avon who?

Avon to drink your blood!

Knock, knock...

Who's there?

Jess.

Jess who?

Jess me and my shadow!

Knock, knock...

Who's there?

De Niro.

De Niro who?

De Niro I am to you, the more I like you!

Knock, knock...

Who's there?

Ben.

Ben who?

Ben knocking on this door all morning!

Knock, knock...

Who's there?

Dime.

Dime who?

Dime to tell another knock, knock joke!

Knock, knock...

Who's there?

Ya.

Ya who?

What are you getting so excited about?

Knock, knock...

Who's there?

Mandy.

Mandy who?

Mandy lifeboats!

Knock, knock...

Who's there?

Accordion.

Accordion who?

Accordion to the weather forecast, it's going to rain tomorrow!

Knock, knock...

Who's there?

Omelet.

Omelet who?

Omelet smarter than I look!

Knock, knock...

Who's there?

Chuck.

Chuck who?

Chuck and see if the door is locked!

Knock, knock...

Who's there?

Carlo.

Carlo who?

Carload of junk!

Knock, knock...

Who's there?

Scott.

Scott who?

Scott a creepy look about it, this place. I think it's haunted!

Knock, knock...

Who's there?

Callista.

Callista who?

Callista warm reception?

Knock, knock...

Who's there?

Dakota.

Dakota who?

Dakota is too small!

Knock, knock...

Who's there?

Conyers.

Conyers who?

Conyers please open the door!

Knock, knock...

Who's there?

Aba.

Aba who?

Aba'out turn. Quick march!

Knock, knock...

Who's there?

Don.

Don who?

Don be afraid... look into my eyes... you are feeling sleepy...

Knock, knock...
Who's there?
Batman.
Batman who?
You mean there's more than one?!

Knock, knock...
Who's there?
Butcher.
Butcher who?
Butcher didn't know it was me at the door, did you?

Knock, knock...
Who's there?
Yodel.
Yodel who?
Yodel who to you too! Let's form a yodel duo!

Knock, knock...
Who's there?
Omar.
Omar who?
Omar goodness gracious, wrong door!

Knock, knock...

Who's there?

Oink moo.

Oink moo who?

You are confused, aren't you?!

Knock, knock...

Who's there?

Eamonn.

Eamonn who?

Eamonn a good mood today, can I come in?

Knock, knock ...

Who's there?

Daryl.

Daryl who?

Daryl never be another you!

Knock, knock...

Who's there?

Björn.

Björn who?

Björn to be wild!

Knock, knock...

Who's there?

Hans.

Hans who?

Hans off the table!

Knock, knock...

Who's there?

Rabbit

Rabbit who?

Rabbit up carefully, it's a present!

Knock, knock...

Who's there?

Sally.

Sally who?

Sally-brate the best moments of your life!

Knock, knock...

Who's there?

Dexter.

Dexter who?

Dexter halls with boughs of holly.

Knock, knock...

Who's there?

Olive.

Olive who?

Olive right next door to you!

Knock, knock...

Who's there?

Cattle.

Cattle who?

Cattle purr if you stroke it!

Knock, knock...

Who's there?

Cheese.

Cheese who?

Cheese a cute dog!

Knock, knock...

Who's there?

Luke.

Luke who?

Luke through the keyhole and you'll see!

Knock, knock...

Who's there?

Mary Lee.

Mary Lee who?

Mary Lee, Mary Lee, life is but a dream! Row, row...

Knock, knock...

Who's there?

Arf.

Arf who?

Arf full or arf empty!

Knock, knock...

Who's there?

Mike.

Mike who?

Mike your mind up!

Knock, knock...

Who's there?

Ice cream.

Ice cream who?

Ice cream every time I see a ghost!

Knock, knock...

Who's there?

Canoe.

Canoe who?

Canoe come out and play today?

Knock, knock...

Who's there?

Paul.

Paul who?

Paul up a chair and I'll tell you!

Knock, knock...
Who's there?
Carol.
Carol who?
Carol down the hill, call the police!

Knock, knock...
Who's there?
Chicken.
Chicken who?
Chicken the oven, I can smell burning!

Knock, knock...
Who's there?
Andrew.
Andrew who?
Andrew a picture!

Knock, knock...

Who's there?

Zone.

Zone who?

Zone shadow scares him!

Knock, knock...

Who's there?

U-8.

U-8 who?

U-8 my lunch!

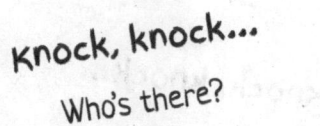

Knock, knock...

Who's there?

Russell.

Russell who?

Russell up a nice hot cup of tea—it's freezing out here!

Knock, knock...

Who's there?

Gopher.

Gopher who?

Gopher help, I'm stuck in the mud!

Knock, knock...

Who's there?

Zookeeper.

Zookeeper who?

Zookeeper away from him!

Knock, knock...

Who's there?

Kline.

Kline who?

Kline of you to invite me round!

Knock, knock...

Who's there?

Kent.

Kent who?

Kent you tell by my voice?

Knock, knock...

Who's there?

Iona.

Iona who?

Iona have eyes for you!

Knock, knock...

Who's there?

Nobel.

Nobel who?

Nobel, that's why I knocked!

Knock, knock...

Who's there?

Farmer.

Farmer who?

Farmer distance your house looks much bigger!

Knock, knock...

Who's there?

Harry.

Harry who?

Harry up! There's a ghost over there!

Knock, knock...

Who's there?

Lionel.

Lionel who?

Lionel bite you if you put your head in its mouth!!!

Knock, knock...

Who's there?

Wade.

Wade who?

Wade down upon the Swanee River!

Knock, knock...

Who's there?

Diana.

Diana who?

Diana of thirst. Can I have a glass of please?

Knock, knock...

Who's there?

Phyllis.

Phyllis who?

Phyllis bucket with water, please!

Knock, knock...

Who's there?

Douglas.

Douglas who?

Douglas is broken!

Knock, knock...

Who's there?

Esau.

Esau who?

Esau you in the bath!

Knock, knock...

Who's there?

Twitter.

Twitter who?

Have you got an owl in there?

Knock, knock...

Who's there?

Cherry.

Cherry who?

Cherry oh, see you later!

Knock, knock...

Who's there?

Duck.

Duck who?

Just duck—they're throwing things at us!

Knock, knock...

Who's there?

Rhoda.

Rhoda who?

Row, Row, Rhoda boat!

Knock, knock...

Who's there?

Peg.

Peg who?

Peg your pardon, I've got the wrong door!

Knock, knock...

Who's there?

Gordy.

Gordy who?

Gordy-rectly to jail, do not pass Go, do not collect da money!

Knock, knock...

Who's there?

Augusta.

Augusta who?

Augusta wind blew my kite away!!

Knock, knock...

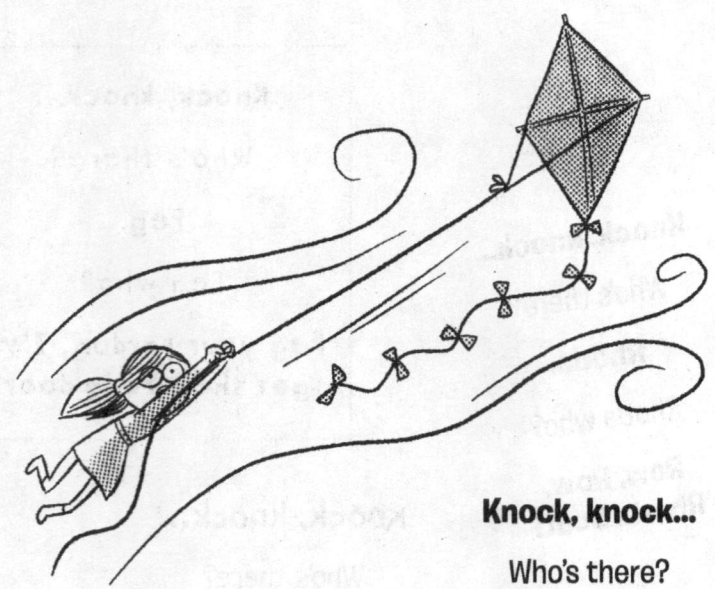

Who's there?

Jim.

Jim who?

Jim mind if I stay here tonight?

Knock, knock...

Who's there?

Aretha.

Aretha who?

Aretha holly on your door.

Knock, knock...

Who's there?

Ivory.

Ivory who?

Ivory strong, just like Tarzan!

Knock, knock...

Who's there?

Hugo.

Hugo who?

Hugo your way and I'll go mine!

Knock, knock...

Who's there?

Fresno.

Fresno who?

Rudolf the Fresno reindeer!

Knock, knock...

Who's there?

Wendy.

Wendy who?

Wendy wind blows de cradle will rock.

Knock, knock...

Who's there?

Larva.

Larva who?

Larva cup of coffee.

Knock, knock...

Who's there?

Eugene.

Eugene who?

Eugene, me Tarzan!

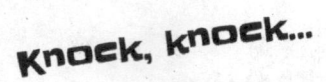

Knock, knock...

Who's there?

Toffee.

Toffee who?

Toffee loved is the best feeling in the world!

Knock, knock...

Who's there?

Dad.

Dad who?

Dad fuel to the fire!

Knock, knock...

Who's there?

Josie.

Josie who?

Josie anyone else out here?

Knock, knock...

Who's there?

Amory.

Amory who?

Amory Christmas!

Knock, knock...

Who's there?

Butter.

Butter who?

Butter bring an umbrella, it looks like it might rain!

Knock, knock...

Who's there?

Lisbon.

Lisbon who?

Lisbon to see me, now she's come to see you!

Knock, knock...

Who's there?

Bernadette.

Bernadette who?

Bernadette all my dinner and now I'm starving!

Knock, knock...

Who's there?

Aunt Lou.

Aunt Lou who?

Aunt Lou do you think you are?

Knock, knock...

Who's there?

Misty.

Misty who?

Misty doorbell again!

Knock, knock...

Who's there?

Donalette.

Donalette who?

Donalette the bed bugs bite!

Knock, knock...

Who's there?

Sam.

Sam who?

Sam-enchanted evening!

Knock, knock...

Who's there?

Aaron.

Aaron who?

Aaron the side of caution!

Knock, knock...

Who's there?

Seymour.

Seymour who?

Seymour of me by opening the door!

Knock, knock...

Who's there?

Wanda.

Wanda who?

Wanda know how much longer you're going to keep me hanging around out here!

Knock, knock...

Who's there?

Kari.

Kari who?

Kari on like this and I'll freeze to death out here!

Knock, knock...

Who's there?

Giraffe.

Giraffe who?

Giraffe to ask me that stupid question?

Knock, knock...

Who's there?

Tank.

Tank who?

You're welcome!

Knock, knock...
Who's there?
Rufus.
Rufus who?
Rufus on fire!

Knock, knock...
Who's there?
Heidi.
Heidi who?
Heidi-clare war on you!

Knock, knock...
Who's there?
Lion.
Lion who?
Lion down on the job again!

Knock, knock...
Who's there?
Police.
Police who?
Police let me in, it's freezing out here!

Knock, knock...

Who's there?

Earl.

Earl who?

Earl be glad to tell you when you open this door!

Knock, knock...

Who's there?

Allied.

Allied who?

Allied, so sue me!

Knock, knock...

Who's there?

Candy.

Candy who?

Candy person who owns this house please open the door!

Knock, knock...

Who's there?

A little girl.

A little girl who?

A little girl who can't reach the doorbell!

Knock, knock...

Who's there?

Cash.

Cash who?

I knew you were nuts!

Knock, knock...

Who's there?

Patty O.

Patty O who?

Patty O furniture!

Knock, knock...

Who's there?

Eyesore.

Eyesore who?

Eyesore do like you!

Knock, knock...

Who's there?

Candace.

Candace who?

Candace be true?

Knock, knock...

Who's there?

Sherwood.

Sherwood who?

Sherwood like to meet you!

Knock, knock...

Who's there?

Diploma.

Diploma who?

Diploma to fix the leak!

Knock, knock...

Who's there?

Aware.

Aware who?

Aware, aware has my little dog gone?

Knock, knock...

Who's there?

Bean.

Bean who?

Bean fishing lately?

Knock, knock...

Who's there?

Hedda.

Hedda who?

Hedda Nuff! I'm bored of waiting!

Knock, knock...

Who's there?

Sarah.

Sarah who?

Sarah bell on this door? I've been knocking for ages!

Knock, knock...

Who's there?

Zeke.

Zeke who?

Zeke and you will find!

Knock, knock...

Who's there?

Lucretia.

Lucretia who?

Lucretia from the Black Lagoon!

Knock, knock...

Who's there?

Paul.

Paul who?

Paul the other one, it's got bells on!

Knock, knock...

Who's there?

Anthem.

Anthem who?

Anthem prince seeking pretty princess.

Knock, knock...

Who's there?

Yachts.

Yachts who?

Yachts up, doc?

Knock, knock...

Who's there?

Wendy.

Wendy who?

Wendy you want me to call round again?

Knock, knock...

Who's there?

Josie.

Josie who?

Josie any reason to keep me waiting out here?

Knock, knock...

Who's there?

Phyllis.

Phyllis who?

Phyllis glass with water, please!

Knock, knock...

Who's there?

Anka.

Anka who?

Anka the ship!

Knock, knock...

Who's there?

Thumping.

Thumping who?

Thumping green and slimy is crawling up your back!

Knock, knock...

Who's there?

Theodore.

Theodore who?

Theodore is stuck and it won't open!

Knock, knock...

Who's there?

Ella.

Ella who?

Ella-vator. Doesn't that give you a lift?

Knock, knock...

Who's there?

Galway.

Galway who?

Galway, you're annoying me!

Knock, knock...

Who's there?

Thayer.

Thayer who?

Thayer thorry or I'll throw thith pie in your face!

Knock, knock...

Who's there?

Ford.

Ford who?

Ford he's a jolly good fellow!

Knock, knock...

Who's there?

Alison.

Alison who?

Alison at the keyhole sometimes!

67

Knock, knock...

Who's there?

Candy.

Candy who?

Candy owner of this big red car come and move it off my driveway!

Knock, knock...

Who's there?

Cy.

Cy who?

Cy'n on the dotted line!

Knock, knock...

Who's there?

Glasgow.

Glasgow who?

Glasgow to the movies!

Knock, knock...

Who's there?

Karl.

Karl who?

I'll Karl again another day when you're feeling better!

Knock, knock...

Who's there?

Kay.

Kay who?

Kay, L, M, N, O, P, Q, R, S, T, U, V, W, X, Y, Z!

Knock, knock...

Who's there?

Anita.

Anita who?

Anita you like I need a hole in the head!

Knock, knock...

Who's there?

Carmen.

Carmen who?

Carmen like best is a Ferrari!

Knock, knock...

Who's there?

Dwayne.

Dwayne who?

Dwayne the bathtub, it's overflowing!

Knock, knock...

Who's there?

Derek.

Derek who?

Derek get richer and de poor get poorer!

Knock, knock...

Who's there?

Felix.

Felix who?

Felix my ice lolly, I'll lick his!

Knock, knock...

Who's there?

Teddy.

Teddy who?

Teddy is the beginning of the rest of your life!

Knock, knock...

Who's there?

Abe.

Abe who?

Abe-C-D-E!

Knock, knock...

Who's there?

Anita.

Anita who?

Anita borrow a pencil!

Knock, knock...

Who's there?

Havelock.

Havelock who?

Havelock put on your door!

Knock, knock...

Who's there?

Fangs.

Fangs who?

Fangs for the memory!

Knock, knock...

Who's there?

Icon.

Icon who?

Icon tell you another knock, knock joke if you want me to!

Knock, knock...

Who's there?

Turner.

Turner who?

Turner round, there's a beautiful view!

Knock, knock...

Who's there?

Earl

Earl who?

Earl-y bird gets the worm!

Knock, knock...

Who's there?

Abbey.

Abbey who?

Abbey stung me on the nose!

Knock, knock...

Who's there?

Madrid.

Madrid who?

Ma-drid you wash my jeans?

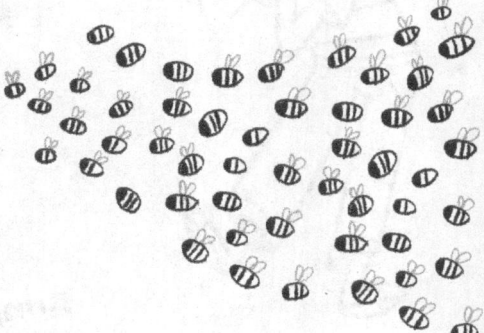

Knock, knock...

Who's there?

Howard.

Howard who?

Howard is it to recognize my voice? I'm your best friend!

Knock, knock...

Who's there?

Dunce.

Dunce who?

Dunce-ay another word!

Knock, knock...

Who's there?

Tom Sawyer.

Tom Sawyer who?

Tom Sawyer underwear!

Knock, knock...

Who's there?

Annie.

Annie who?

Annie way can you let me in?

Knock, knock...

Who's there?

Ike.

Ike who?

Ike can't stop laughing!

Knock, knock...

Who's there?

Just Paul.

Just Paul who?

Just Pauling your leg — it's Steve really!

Knock, knock...
Who's there?
Egbert.
Egbert who?
Egbert no bacon!

Knock, knock...
Who's there?
Sacha.
Sacha who?
Sacha fuss over nothing!

Knock, knock...
Who's there?
Althea.
Althea who?
Althea later, alligator!

Knock, knock...
Who's there?
Alice.
Alice who?
Alice is fair in love and war!

Knock, knock...

Who's there?

Closure.

Closure who?

Closure mouth when you're eating!

Knock, knock...

Who's there?

Brigham.

Brigham who?

Brigham back my sunshine to me!

Knock, knock...

Who's there?

Belize.

Belize who?

Belize in yourself!

Knock, knock...

Who's there?

Icing.

Icing who?

Icing carols—you give me money!

Knock, knock...

Who's there?

Blue.

Blue who?

Blue away with the wind!

Knock, knock...

Who's there?

Julia.

Julia who?

Julia want some milk and cookies?

Knock, knock...

Who's there?

Telly.

Telly who?

Telly your friend to come out!

Knock, knock...

Who's there?

Yvette.

Yvette who?

Yvette helps lots of animals.

Knock, knock...

Who's there?

Amy.

Amy who?

Amy fraid I've forgotten!

Knock, knock...

Who's there?

Lauren.

Lauren who?

Lauren order!

Knock, knock...

Who's there?

Waddle.

Waddle who?

Waddle you give me if I promise to go away?

Knock, knock...

Who's there?

Carol.

Carol who?

Carol go if you fill it with fuel!

Knock, knock...

Who's there?

Cohen.

Cohen who?

Cohen to knock just once more, then I'm going away!

Knock, knock...

Who's there?

Desiree.

Desiree who?

Desiree of sunshine in my life!

Knock, knock...

Who's there?

Sam.

Sam who?

Sam person who knocked on the door last time!

Knock, knock...

Who's there?

Brewster.

Brewster who?

Brewster wakes me up every morning singing cock-a-doodle-do!

Knock, knock...
Who's there?
Cole.
Cole who?
Cole as a cucumber!

Knock, knock...
Who's there?
Guthrie.
Guthrie who?
Guthrie blind mice!

Knock, knock...
Who's there?
Champ.
Champ who?
Champ-oo in my eyes. I can't see!

Knock, knock...
Who's there?
Pasture.
Pasture who?
Pasture bedtime, isn't it?

Knock, knock...
Who's there?
Denis.
Denis who?
Denis anyone?

Knock, knock...
Who's there?
Harry.
Harry who?
Harry you been?

Knock, knock...
Who's there?
Cass.
Cass who?
Cass more flies with honey than vinegar!

Knock, knock...
Who's there?
Jess.
Jess who?
I give up, who?

Knock, knock...
Who's there?
Venice.
Venice who?
Venice this door going to open?

Knock, knock...
Who's there?
Ivan.
Ivan who?
Ivan infectious disease, so watch out!

Knock, knock...
Who's there?
Curry.
Curry who?
Curry me back home will you?

Knock, knock...
Who's there?
Jester.
Jester who?
Jester minute, I'm trying to find my keys!

Knock, knock...

Who's there?

Gorilla.

Gorilla who?

Gorilla cheese sandwich for me and I'll be right over!

Knock, knock...

Who's there?

Costas.

Costas who?

Costas a fortune to get here!

Knock, knock...

Who's there?

Aki.

Aki who?

Aki would be really useful right now!

Knock, knock...

Who's there?

Ethan.

Ethan who?

Ethan me out of house and home, you are!

Knock, knock...

Who's there?

Handsome.

Handsome who?

Handsome money through the keyhole and I'll tell you more!

Knock, knock...

Who's there?

Frank.

Frank who?

Frankenstein!

Knock, knock...

Who's there?

Grant.

Grant who?

Grant you a wish, what is it?

Knock, knock...

Who's there?

Chris.

Chris who?

Christmas is coming and the goose is getting fat!

Knock, knock...

Who's there?

Izzy.

Izzy who?

Izzy come, Izzy go!

Knock, knock...

Who's there?

May.

May who?

May the force be with you!

Knock, knock...

Who's there?

Henrietta.

Henrietta who?

Henrietta worm that was in his apple!

Knock, knock...

Who's there?

Carla.

Carla who?

Carla taxi, I'm leaving!

Knock, knock...

Who's there?

Deduct.

Deduct who?

Donald Deduct!

Knock, knock...

Who's there?

Andy.

Andy who?

Andy mosquito bit me again!

Knock, knock...

Who's there?

Moo.

Moo who?

Well, make up your mind, are you a cow or an owl?

Knock, knock...

Who's there?

Alfalfa.

Alfalfa who?

Alfalfa you, if you give me a kiss!

Knock, knock...

Who's there?

Genoa.

Genoa who?

Genoa any new jokes?

Knock, knock...

Who's there?

Parson.

Parson who?

Parson through and I thought I'd say hello!

Knock, knock...

Who's there?

Rita.

Rita who?

Rita book, you might learn something!

Knock, knock...

Who's there?

Muffin.

Muffin who?

Muffin the matter with me. How about you?

Knock, knock...

Who's there?

Hannah.

Hannah who?

Hannah partridge in a pear tree!

Knock, knock...

Who's there?

Havana.

Havana who?

Havana wonderful time, wish you were here!

Knock, knock...

Who's there?

Jacklyn.

Jacklyn who?

Jacklyn Hyde!

Knock, knock...

Who's there?

Morse.

Morse who?

Morse come in as quickly as possible!

Knock, knock...

Who's there?

Toby.

Toby who?

Toby or not to be!

Knock, knock...

Who's there?

Dill.

Dill who?

Dill we meet again!

Knock, knock...

Who's there?

Gin.

Gin who?

Gin know how cold it is out here?

Knock, knock...

Who's there?

Butcher.

Butcher who?

Butcher said I could come and visit you!

Knock, knock...

Who's there?

Enid.

Enid who?

Enid some more money!

Knock, knock...

Who's there?

Donatello.

Donatello who?

Donatello'n me!

Knock, knock...

Who's there?

Harriet.

Harriet who?

Harriet up!

Knock, knock...

Who's there?

Norma Lee.

Norma Lee who?

Norma Lee I don't go around knocking on doors, but do you want your windows cleaned?

Knock, knock...

Who's there?

Alaska.

Alaska who?

Alaska again, please open the door!

Knock, knock...

Who's there?

Betty.

Betty who?

Betty ya don't know who this is!

Knock, knock...

Who's there?

Don.

Don who?

Don Patrol!

Knock, knock...

Who's there?

Teacher.

Teacher who?

Teacher self for a few days. I'm having a break!

Knock, knock...

Who's there?

Apple.

Apple who?

Apple your hair if you don't let me in!

Knock, knock...

Who's there?

Arch.

Arch who?

Are you catching a cold?

Knock, knock...

Who's there?

Carrie.

Carrie who?

Carrie the bags into the house please!

Knock, knock...

Who's there?

Elvis.

Elvis who?

Elvis is a complete waste of time, I'm off!

Knock, knock...

Who's there?

Hippo.

Hippo who?

Hippo-hop, dance till I drop!

Knock, knock...

Who's there?

Otto.

Otto who?

Ottold you two seconds ago!

Knock, knock...

Who's there?

Sid.

Sid who?

Sid you'd be ready by three— where are you?!

Knock, knock...

Who's there?

Cello.

Cello who?

Cello, how are you?

Knock, knock...

Who's there?

Belle.

Belle who?

Belle doesn't work, so I'm having to knock!

Knock, knock...

Who's there?

Haydn.

Haydn who?

Haydn in this cupboard is boring!

Knock, knock...

Who's there?

Cereal.

Cereal who?

Cereal pleasure to meet you!

Knock, knock...

Who's there?

Scold.

Scold who?

Scold outside.

Knock, knock...

Who's there?

Olivia.

Olivia who?

Olivia, so get out of my house!

Knock, knock...

Who's there?

Ferdie.

Ferdie who?

Ferdie last time, open this door!

Knock, knock...

Who's there?

Figs.

Figs who?

Figs the doorbell, it's broken!

Knock, knock...

Who's there?

Chuck.

Chuck who?

Chuck the key under the door and I'll let myself in!

Knock, knock...

Who's there?

Pearce.

Pearce who?

Pearce this balloon with a pin!

Knock, knock...

Who's there?

Oliver.

Oliver who?

Oliver cross the road from you!

Knock, knock...

Who's there?

Posh.

Posh who?

Posh the door open and you'll see!

Knock, knock...

Who's there?

Amanda.

Amanda who?

Amanda fix the boiler!

Knock, knock...

Who's there?

Yubin.

Yubin who?

Yubin eating garlic again?

Knock, knock...

Who's there?

Boo.

Boo who?

Bootiful front door you have.

Knock, knock...

Who's there?

Ben.

Ben who?

Ben wondering what you're up to!

Knock, knock...

Who's there?

Alfie.

Alfie who?

Alfie terrible if you leave!

Knock, knock...

Who's there?

Leena.

Leena who?

Leena little closer and I'll whisper in your ear!

Knock, knock...

Who's there?

Chimney.

Chimney who?

Chimney cricket! Have you seen Pinocchio?

Knock, knock...

Who's there?

Fletch.

Fletch who?

Fletch the firefighters, the house is on fire!

Knock, knock...

Who's there?

Hawaii.

Hawaii who?

I'm fine, Hawaii you?

Knock, knock...

Who's there?

Harmon.

Harmon who?

Harmon your side!

Knock, knock...

Who's there?

Snow.

Snow who?

Snow use, I've lost my key again!

Knock, knock...

Who's there?

Yogurt.

Yogurt who?

Yogurt to love my jokes!

Knock, knock...

Who's there

Zeb.

Zeb who?

Zeb better be a good reason for keeping me waiting out here!

Knock, knock...

Who's there?

Oman.

Oman who?

Oman, you are cute!

Knock, knock...
Who's there?
Caesar.
Caesar who?
Caesar jolly good fellow!

Knock, knock...
Who's there?
Dale.
Dale who?
Dale come if you ask dem!

Knock, knock...
Who's there?
Boo.
Boo who?
Don't be scared, it's only a game!

Knock, knock...
Who's there?
Harold.
Harold who?
Harold are you?

Knock, knock...
Who's there?
Vassar.
Vassar who?
Vassar girl like you doing in a place like this?

Knock, knock...
Who's there?
Eileen.
Eileen who?
Eileen down to tie my shoe!

Knock, knock...
Who's there?
Mary.
Mary who?
Mary Christmas, ho, ho, ho!

Knock, knock...
Who's there?
Custer.
Custer who?
Custer lot to find out!

Knock, knock...

Who's there?

Patrick.

Patrick who?

Patricked me into knocking on your door!

Knock, knock...

Who's there?

Argue.

Argue who?

Argue going to let me in or not?

Knock, knock...

Who's there?

Alpaca.

Alpaca who?

Alpaca the bag, you packa the suitcase!

Knock, knock...

Who's there?

Congo.

Congo who?

Congo near a volcano, it's dangerous!

Knock, knock...

Who's there?

Howard.

Howard who?

Howard you know if you won't even open the door?

Knock, knock...

Who's there?

Betty.

Betty who?

Betty earns a lot of money!

Knock, knock...
Who's there?
Ezra.
Ezra who?
Ezra no hope for me?

Knock, knock...
Who's there?
Turkey.
Turkey who?
Turkey and find out!

Knock, knock...
Who's there?
Zany.
Zany who?
Zany body home?

Knock, knock...
Who's there?
Bacon.
Bacon who?
Bacon a cake for your birthday!

Knock, knock...

Who's there?

A man.

A man who?

A man with a wooden leg.

Tell him to hop it!

Knock, knock...

Who's there?

Amish.

Amish who?

Amish you too!

Knock, knock...

Who's there?

Shelby.

Shelby who?

Shelby coming round the mountain when she comes!

Knock, knock...

Who's there?

You.

You who?

You-who to you, too!

Knock, knock...

Who's there?

Hank.

Hank who?

Hank you!

Knock, knock...

Who's there?

Pat.

Pat who?

Pat yourself on the back!

Knock, knock...

Who's there?

Little old lady.

Little old lady who?

Your yodeling's getting much better!

Knock, knock...
Who's there?
Wooden shoe.
Wooden shoe who?
Wooden shoe like to hear another joke?

Knock, knock...
Who's there?
Gopher.
Gopher who?
Gopher broke!

Knock, knock...
Who's there?
Gable.
Gable who?
Gable to leap buildings in a single bound!

Knock, knock...
Who's there?
Eva.
Eva who?
Eva you're not listening or your doorbell isn't working!

Knock, knock...

Who's there?

Ben.

Ben who?

Ben down and tie your shoelaces!

Knock, knock...

Who's there?

Cora.

Cora who?

Cora wish I had a front door like this!

Knock, knock...

Who's there?

Isadore.

Isadore who?

Isadore on the right way round?

Knock, knock...

Who's there?

Daisy.

Daisy who?

Daisy plays, nights he sleeps!

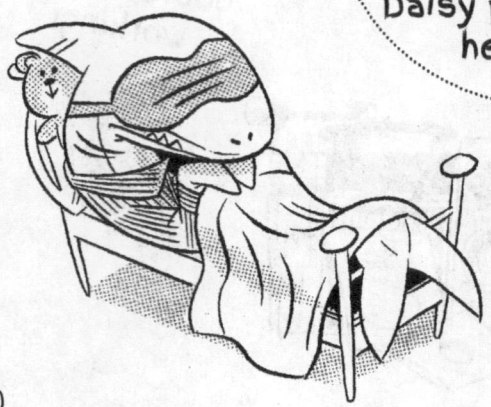

Knock, knock...

Who's there?

Sonia.

Sonia who?

Sonia shoe. I can smell it from here.

Knock, knock...

Who's there?

Aardvark.

Aardvark who?

Aardvark a million miles for one of your smiles!

Knock, knock...

Who's there?

Dishes.

Dishes who?

Dishes the police! Open up!

Knock, knock...

Who's there?

C-2.

C-2 who?

C-2 it that you don't forget my name next time!

Knock, knock...

Who's there?

Chad.

Chad who?

Chad to make your acquaintance!

Knock, knock...

Who's there?

Guess Simon.

Guess Simon who?

Guess Simon the wrong doorstep!

Knock, knock...

Who's there?

Mike.

Mike who?

Mike car won't start, can I come in and use the phone?

Knock, knock...

Who's there?

Cathy.

Cathy who?

Cathy the doorbell, it's too dark out here!

Knock, knock...

Who's there?

Jerome.

Jerome who?

Jerome at last!

Knock, knock...

Who's there?

I-8.

I-8 who?

I-8 lunch already... When is dinner?

Knock, knock...

Who's there?

Cynthia.

Cynthia who?

Cynthia been away I've missed you!

Knock, knock...

Who's there?

Postman Pat.

Have you got a parcel?

No, but I've got a black and white cat!

Knock, knock...

Who's there?

Khan.

Khan who?

Khan you give me a ride to school?

Knock, knock...

Who's there?

Emma.

Emma who?

Emma bit cold out here, can you let me in?

Knock, knock...

Who's there?

Darwin.

Darwin who?

I'll be Darwin you open the door!

Knock, knock...

Who's there?

Darren.

Darren who?

Darren people in their flying machines!

Knock, knock...

Who's there?

Germany.

Germany who?

Germany people knock on your door?

Knock, knock...

Who's there?

Disguise.

Disguise who?

Disguise the limit!

Knock, knock...

Who's there?

Gandhi.

Gandhi who?

Gandhi cane!

Knock, knock...

Who's there?

Adair.

Adair who?

Adair once, but I'm bald now!

Knock, knock...

Who's there?

Anna.

Anna who?

Anna gonna tell you!

Knock, knock...

Who's there?

Avenue.

Avenue who?

Avenue guessed yet?

Knock, knock...

Who's there?

Ahab.

Ahab who?

Ahab to go to the bathroom. Quick, open the door!

Knock, knock...
Who's there?
Amos.
Amos who?
Amosquito just bit me!

Knock, knock...
Who's there?
CD.
CD who?
CDs fingers? They're freezing—let me in!

Knock, knock
Who's there?
Waiter.
Waiter who?
Waiter minute, this isn't my house!

Knock, knock...
Who's there?
Aida.
Aida who?
Aida lot of chocolates and now I've got a stomach ache!

Knock, knock...

Who's there?

Red.

Red who?

Red your letters, you can have them back now!

Knock, knock...

Who's there?

Edwin.

Edwin who?

Edwin a cup if he could run faster!

Knock, knock...

Who's there?

Dublin.

Dublin who?

Dublin up with laughter!

Knock, knock...

Who's there?

Alex.

Alex who?

Alex the questions round here!

Knock, knock...

Who's there?

Barbara.

Barbara who?

Barbara black sheep!

Knock, knock...

Who's there?

Atlas.

Atlas who?

Atlas it's the weekend!

Knock, knock...

Who's there?

Amanda.

Amanda who?

Amanda the table!

Knock, knock...

Who's there?

Adolf.

Adolf who?

Adolf ball hit me in de mouf!

Knock, knock...

Who's there?

Homer.

Homer who?

Homer goodness! I can't remember my name!

Knock, knock...

Who's there?

Delhi.

Delhi who?

Delhicatessen!

Knock, knock...

Who's there?

Ethan.

Ethan who?

Ethan too much makes you feel awful!

Knock, knock...

Who's there?

Nana.

Nana who?

Nana your business!

Knock, knock...

Who's there?

Alec.

Alec who?

Alec-tricity. Isn't that a shock?

Knock, knock...

Who's there?

Thermos.

Thermos who?

Thermos be a better knock, knock joke than this!

Knock, knock...

Who's there?

Ferrer.

Ferrer who?

Ferrer'vrything there is a season!

Knock, knock...

Who's there?

Perth.

Perth who?

Perth your lips and whistle!

Knock, knock...

Who's there?

Bill.

Bill who?

Bill-ding's on fire!

Knock, knock...

Who's there?

Baby.

Baby who?

Baby I shouldn't hab come round wiv dis cold!

Knock, knock...

Who's there?

Munchin.

Munchin who?

Munchin my dinner and need a drink.

Knock, knock...

Who's there?

Berlin.

Berlin who?

Berlin the water for my hard-boiled eggs!

Knock, knock...

Who's there?

Edith.

Edith who?

Edith, it'll make you feel better!

Knock, knock...

Who's there?

Ear.

Ear who?

Ear you are! I've been looking for you!

Knock, knock...

Who's there?

Water.

Water who?

Water you doing in my house?

Knock, knock...

Who's there?

Carl.

Carl who?

Carl get you there quicker than if you walk!

Knock, knock...

Who's there?

Jester.

Jester who?

Jester day, you were out. Today, you're in!

Knock, knock...

Who's there?

McKee.

McKee who?

McKee doesn't fit!

Knock, knock...

Who's there?

Haden.

Haden who?

Haden seek!

Knock, knock...

Who's there?

Amahl.

Amahl who?

Amahl shook up!

Knock, knock...

Who's there?

Indy.

Indy who?

Indy hallway is some of my stuff, and I've come to collect it!

Knock, knock...

Who's there?

Beezer.

Beezer who?

Beezer black and yellow and make honey!

Knock, knock...
Who's there?
The Vampire.
The Vampire who?
The Vampire State Building!

Knock, knock...
Who's there?
Element.
Element who?
Element to tell you that she can't see you today!

Knock, knock...
Who's there?
Wood.
Wood who?
Wood you like to let me in now?

Knock, knock...
Who's there?
Scott.
Scott who?
Scott nothing to do with you!

Knock, knock...

Who's there?

Alva.

Alva who?

Alva heart!

Knock, knock...

Who's there?

Jack.

Jack who?

Jackpot! We've won first prize!

Knock, knock...

Who's there?

Dragon.

Dragon who?

Dragon your feet again!

Knock, knock...

Who's there?

Ida.

Ida who?

Ida run fast if a dinosaur was chasing me!

Knock, knock...
Who's there?
Jez.
Jez who?
Jez me, that's who!

Knock, knock...
Who's there?
Snow.
Snow who?
Snow use — I can't remember!

Knock, knock...
Who's there?
Tuna.
Tuna who?
Tuna whole orchestra!

Knock, knock...
Who's there?
Brad.
Brad who?
Brad news, I'm afraid —this is the last knock, knock joke!